I Feel...

LONELY

Words and pictures by

DJ Corchin

sourcebooks
eXplore

Sometimes I feel **lonely**.

Like I don't have a **friend**.

So I head to my room

and start to **pretend**.

I **take off** in a rocket

or **swim** under the sea.

I practice my **magic**

and **fly** as far as can be.

I might even suggest
that the trip just be **me**.

But secretly I wish you would **join** me for tea.

Sometimes I get **quiet**.

Sometimes I **act out**.

Sometimes I'm so **scared** that I scream and I shout.

Or I might find a corner
and sit there and **pout**.

With my **imaginary** friend and her specular snout.

Sometimes I get **sad**.

And **ponder** and think.

Or **stare off** into space.

And won't even **blink.**

Sometimes I can feel like I'm way **out of sync**.

So I **write** in my journal
'til I run out of ink.

Sometimes I can feel like I'm all **on my own**.

In **my own** little world
on my own little throne.

But no matter how long
I think this **feeling** will last,

I know I'm **OK** 'cause this feeling will pass.

I Feel...
LONELY

It's OK to want to be alone for a bit, but not for too long. When you feel lonely, what can you do?

Feeling lonely can come along with so many other emotions including anger, sadness, or fear. Sometimes, we want to be left alone and have our own space.

Sometimes we may feel lonely, but still be surrounded by those who love us. It can be hard to tell why you might be feeling lonely. Here are some activities to help when you're feeling that way.

Make a Caring Tree

1. What's a caring tree? This is even bigger than a family tree. This is a family tree PLUS extra branches for all the other caring adults and friends that you have in your life. Maybe it isn't even in the shape of a tree. Maybe you have more of a caring web. Or a caring Ferris wheel? It's completely up to you!

2. Make a list of as many friends and family members you can think of. You can start a conversation with a family member about your family tree. Include people you know whom you trust or feel good about talking to. This list can be anyone! A teacher you love? Yes. A special coach? Of course. Your best friend? Add them.

3. Using colored paper, cut out heart shapes—one for every person on your special caring list. You can make them different sizes for adults and kids.

4. Draw I Feel... faces on them using this book as an example of how to draw different expressions.

5. Write the person's name above each I Feel... face.

6. Below their face, describe why you enjoy being around this person and the things that make them wonderful. If you miss them, write what you miss most about seeing them.

7. You can glue the hearts to a large piece of paper or ask a parent or guardian if you can tape them to your wall or a door.

8. When you feel lonely, you can look at all the people who care about you and remember that even when you're not together, they're thinking about you too.

Start an I Feel... Pen Pal Exchange

Everyone feels lonely sometimes. It can help to reach out to others and send them something in the mail. You might get something back in return!

1. Draw yourself as an I Feel... face using whatever shape you would like.

2. Glue it to a piece of paper and write about yourself on the side. You could write:

   What your favorite colors are

   Where you live

   If you have any pets

   Fun activities you like

3. Mail your letter to a friend or family member asking if they'd like to be your pen pal. If so, ask them to write back with their own I Feel... face and a little bit of information about themselves.

4. Don't forget to draw a fun I Feel... face on the envelope so they know it's from you!

I Feel...like doing something! Activity Cards

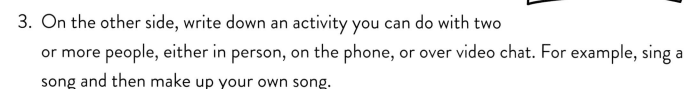

1. Use a pack of plain index cards, or cut blank paper to 4" x 6" rectangles. You can start with ten and then add more cards as you add more activities.

2. On one side, draw fun I Feel... faces using any shape you wish. Try drawing different expressions.

3. On the other side, write down an activity you can do with two or more people, either in person, on the phone, or over video chat. For example, sing a song and then make up your own song.

4. If you want to, you can color the back side of the card one color for outdoor activities and another color for indoors.

5. When you're feeling lonely, pick a card and connect with a friend or family member to do the activity and have some fun!

Remember: You're never really alone even if you feel that way. It's important to reach out to a caring adult when you're feeling sad or lonely.

It is ALWAYS OK to ask someone for help when you are feeling bad.

The I Feel... Children's Series is a resource created to assist in discussions about emotional awareness.

Please seek the help of a trained mental healthcare professional and start a discussion today.

To Sam

Published by Sourcebooks eXplore, an imprint of Sourcebooks Kids
P.O. Box 4410, Naperville, Illinois 60567–4410
(630) 961-3900
sourcebookskids.com

Originally published in 2017 in the United States of America by The phazelFOZ Company, LLC.

Library of Congress Cataloging-in-Publication Data is on file with the publisher.

Source of Production: 1010 Printing Asia Limited, North Point, Hong Kong, China
Date of Production: July 2020
Run Number: 5019063

Printed and bound in China.
OGP 10 9 8 7 6 5 4 3 2 1